The Patchsmith's

ANIMAL and PET MUG RUGS

by Amanda Weatherill

CONTENTS

General Instructions

Before you start
Read through all instructions for the pattern of your choice before beginning.
Fabric requirements and cutting directions are given at the beginning of each pattern.
All seam allowances are ¼" and are included in cutting sizes.
Press seam allowance towards the darker fabric unless stated otherwise.

Using the patterns
Each pattern has been created as a stand-alone unit to allow you to work quickly and easily. The appliqué diagrams are located with the individual patterns and are at the correct size. Some of the appliqué images have been reversed – you should trace them exactly as shown on the appliqué page – they will be the right way round on your finished mug rug.

Fabric Choices
Choosing your fabrics can often taken longer than making the actual mug rug and this is true whether choosing from a designer range or using up scraps left over from a bigger project. The largest piece of fabric you will require for any of the projects in this book is 11" x 8" and that is for the backing - the appliqué detailing uses much smaller pieces. Before you start, make sure any fabric you use is colour-fast (you can test it by soaking a small piece in a bowl of water – the water should remain clear).

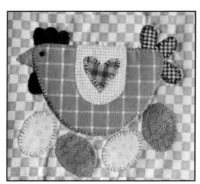

If you are new to mug rugs or small quilts then a good way to build up a fabric stash is to use pre-cuts i.e. charm packs and layer cakes. These can be found in most quilting and fabric shops. It is also handy to have a few fat-quarters (quarter of a yard) ready for background and backing. A good background fabric will have a small print and not be too bold in design or colour.

Do not neglect the back of your mug rug. This is particularly important if you are creating the mug rug as a gift. Try to choose a backing fabric that will complement the front of the mug rug. Novelty fabrics work well – especially with animal mug rugs.

Mug rugs are meant to be fun – they give you the opportunity to play with pattern and colour – so remember this and try out some unusual combinations. You never know when you'll discover a new favourite group of colours or pattern.

Appliqué

All patterns in this book use the quick and easy fusible method of appliqué. You will need lightweight fusible webbing (i.e. Bondaweb, Vleisofix, Wonderweb or similar). Each pattern includes appliqué instructions but here they are in a little more detail:

1.   Trace around the appliqué shapes onto the paper side of the fusible webbing. Fusible webbing has two sides – one smooth (paper side) and one rough (webbing side). Trace the design onto the smooth paper side.
Note: Some of the shapes have been reversed – trace them exactly as shown.

2.   Cut out the shapes roughly (do not cut out accurately at this stage). You should leave approximately ¼" free around each shape when cutting out.

3.   Follow the manufacturer's instructions to iron the fusible webbing cut outs onto the WRONG side of your chosen fabrics. The rough (webbing) side should be facing the WRONG side of your fabric and you will be ironing the paper side. DO NOT IRON THE WEBBING SIDE – YOU WILL RUIN YOUR IRON.

4.   Allow the fabric to cool completely before cutting out the shapes accurately along the traced lines.

5.   Peel the paper away from the fusible webbing/fabric.

Tip: *If you have difficulty peeling the paper away from the fabric, scratch the paper gently with a pin until you create a tear in the paper. Slide the pin between the fabric and paper. You should then be able to remove it easily.*

This will leave a layer of glue on the fabric cut outs. Position the fabric cut outs, with the glue side facing down, onto the RIGHT side of the mug rug. Use the appliqué page and photo as a guide to their placement and make a note of any pieces which overlap. When happy with the arrangement, fuse the pieces in place according to manufacturer's instructions.

TIP: *Always leave enough room between the appliqué and the edge of the mug rug to allow for binding.*

6.   Finally stitch the appliqué shapes securely in place by hand or machine. You can use a running stitch, blanket stitch or any decorative stitch you prefer. It is important to stitch the pieces so that they do not come off when the mug rug is laundered.

Quilting

Mug rugs can be quilted with any thick material you have to hand – it doesn't have to be batting or wadding. You can use old towelling, wool fabric, flannel or interfacing. Whatever you use though should be washable and thick enough to protect the table from hot cups/liquid. I use both natural and synthetic materials ranging in thickness from 2 oz to 4 oz.

When it comes to quilting the finished mug rug, you can make it as simple or as complex as you like, whether by machine or by hand. You can even leave the mug rug un-quilted if you wish.

To prepare your mug rug for quilting, lay the backing material with WRONG side facing up, lay the batting on top and finally lay the mug rug with RIGHT side facing up on top of both. (In effect you have a sandwich of batting between the backing material and the mug rug top.) Baste or pin all three layers together, ensuring that the backing and top remain flat and smooth. Quilt as preferred (hand or machine) and quilt around any appliqué shapes.

Tip: The closer your quilting is to the appliqué shape will determine how 'puffed up' the appliqué is. Try stitching very close (almost touching) and then try ⅛" away on another mug rug and see the difference.

Once all quilting has been completed, trim the backing and batting level with the mug rug top.

Binding Methods

There are many different ways to finish your mug rugs. For all the patterns within this book I have used 1¼" wide cotton strips for binding but you could use bias binding if you prefer. I do not cut my binding on the bias unless I want a particular look i.e. a diagonal stripe. All binding is cut from ordinary quilters' cotton fabric.

You can use any binding method you are familiar with or prefer. There are some excellent tutorials on-line for machine and hand binding. I have given instructions here for simple 'single fold' and mitred binding.

Single Fold Binding

1.   Cut four binding strips each measuring 2" longer than the sides of your mug rug i.e. if your mug rug is 6" x 9" cut two 8" and two 11" strips.

2.   With RIGHT sides together stitch a binding strip to the top and bottom of your mug rug. Trim excess binding to match width of mug rug. Press the binding away from the mug rug.

3.   Repeat with the two remaining binding strips to the sides of the mug rug. Trim excess binding to match length of mug rug. Press the binding away from the mug rug.

4.   Fold the binding round to the back of the rug. Turn under ¼" on the outside edge of the binding and slip stitch the binding in place. Be careful not to stitch through to the front of the rug.

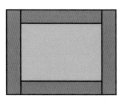
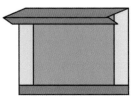

With RIGHT sides together stitch the binding to the top and bottom of the mug rug. Trim the binding to the same width as the mug rug.

Press the binding away from the mug rug.

Repeat for the sides.

Turn binding to the back of the mug rug, turn under ¼" and slip-stitch in place. Repeat for all sides.

Mitred Binding

This method of binding creates a mitred corner finish for your mug rug.
Note: You will need one continuous length of 1¼" wide binding – this can be constructed from strips sewn together.

1. Fold the short end of your binding strip into a triangle and align to one edge of the mug rug, RIGHT sides together, as shown (this will create a neat start/finish to your binding). Stitch the binding to the side of your mug rug but stop when you are ½" away from the first corner. Cut the thread and take the rug out of the machine.

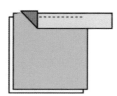

2. Now fold the binding up and away from the mug rug as shown. This will create a triangular fold in the binding at the corner.

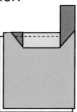

3. Hold the triangular fold (or pin it) before folding the binding down over it, aligning the edge of the binding with the side of the mug rug. Pin to secure in place. Stitch the binding along the side from top to bottom, stopping once again when you are ½" away from the next corner.

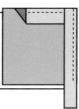

4. Repeat this process for all four corners. Continue stitching the binding until you are 1" past the beginning.

5. Fold binding to the back of the mug rug, turning under ¼" on the raw edge. Slip-stitch in place over the line of machine stitching. Make sure you do not stitch through to the front.

Hanging Corner Triangles

Some mug rugs are so pretty that you may wish to hang one on the wall rather than have it on your table. Or perhaps you already have one on your desk but want to make another. Hanging corner triangles are a great way to achieve this. They enable you to hang a mug rug or small quilt using only one tack in the wall.

All that is needed is two 3" squares of fabric. Fold the squares in half diagonally, with WRONG sides together and press. After quilting and trimming your mug rug and prior to attaching the binding to your mug rug first pin the triangles to the top corners on the back of your quilt.

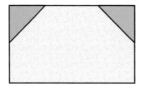 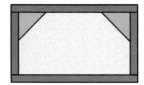

Then complete the binding using the method you prefer. As you stitch the binding in place you will also be stitching the triangles in place.

To hang your mug rug all you need do is insert a pencil or chopstick (trimmed if necessary) into the two corners and hang it on a small tack/nail.

Tip: *To hang a mug rug you have already made, attach a safety pin to the center back of the mug rug and hang it on a nail or tack.*

Ribbons and Trim

Mug rugs are functional mini quilts. Cups and mugs are placed on them along with cookies, cakes and biscuits. Spills and drips are unavoidable and as such, it is important that mug rugs can be laundered. Ribbons, labels and trims can add an extra dimension to little quilts but make sure they are suitable for laundering and ironing before adding them to your quilt.

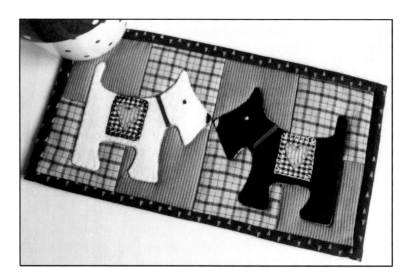

Hints and Tips

Here are a dozen of my top tips for all mug rug makers:

1.　　If you are new to mug rug making or short of time use a single piece of fabric for the background rather than patching the background. You can find the finished size of each mug rug underneath the pattern headings. Cut your single piece of fabric to this size or bigger – you can always trim it down later.

2.　　Read through the pattern completely before starting. Each design in this book works as a stand-alone pattern – you will not have to go backwards and forwards through this book to find the information you need. However, if you are new to mug rug making, the introduction provides more detail regarding the process – read this first before starting the individual patterns.

3.　　Use a neutral background for your mug rug (i.e. cream, beige, grey, or tan). This will make selecting appliqué fabrics easier.

4.　　Use fabrics from a pre-cut pack i.e. a charm pack or layer cake. You can be certain they will blend and go together.

5.　　Let fusible webbing cool completely – it is easier to peel off the paper when it is cold. You may want to get your mug rug finished NOW but go make a cup of tea. By the time you bring your cuppa back to the sewing room the appliqué should be cooled and ready for peeling.

6.   If you have trouble removing the backing paper once it has been fused in place, scratch it carefully with a pin until you can slip the pin between the fabric and the paper.

7.   Do not be afraid to combine methods i.e. hand and machine stitching within the same mug rug.

 8.   When starting out use a plain binding.   Stripes and checks require precision when cutting so that the pattern appears straight.   If in doubt choose a darker fabric for binding as this will frame the mug rug.

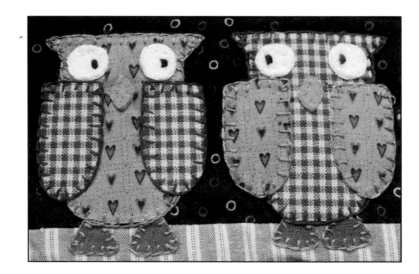

9.   Do not worry about wonky stitches or unmatched seams – only you will notice them. If you are making a mug rug as a gift the recipient will be thrilled that you have taken the time to make something by hand – they really won't notice the odd wonky seam.

10.   Move the fabric, rather than moving the scissors when cutting circles or curves – this will make for a smoother cut (this may sound odd but try it, you'll see what I mean).

11.   Use felt for very small pieces – it won't fray.

12.   Have fun. Mug rugs are primarily about producing a functional little quilt whilst playing with fabric. The most you will ever lose is a few small pieces of fabric and an hour or two of your time. So smile at your mistakes – after all, they are really just learning experiences.

Let us make a start on the patterns.

SPRING LAMBS MUG RUG

(Finished size: 9½" x 5")

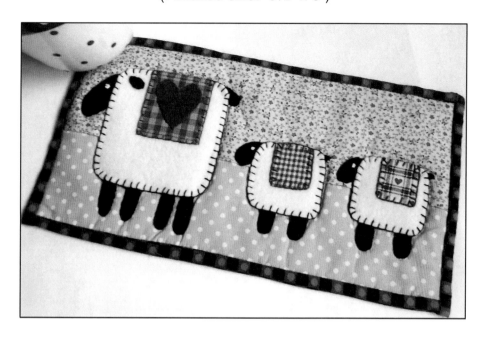

One of the first signs that spring has arrived is when the lambs start appearing in the fields closely following their mother. This Folk Art mug rug, with its cosy country blankets, will bring a touch of spring-time cuteness to your table.

Fabric Requirements:

For the Background:
One 9½" x 2½" rectangle green fabric
One 9½" x 3" rectangle cream/blue fabric

For the Sheep:
One 4" square white felt or thick white cotton fabric for body
One 2" square of fabric for blanket

For the Lambs:
Two 2½" squares of white felt or thick white cotton fabric for bodies
Two 1½" squares of fabric for blankets

You will also need:
Scraps of cotton fabric for heads, legs, ear, tail and heart
One 11" x 7" rectangle of cotton fabric for backing
One 11" x 7" rectangle of lightweight batting
10" square fusible webbing (i.e. Bondaweb/Wonderweb)
1 yard of 1¼" binding fabric (i.e. bias binding or cotton strips)
Stranded Embroidery Cotton

Mug Rug Construction

1.   With RIGHT sides together stitch the two background rectangles together to create a mug rug top which measures 9½" x 5".   Press.

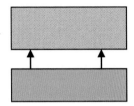

2.   From the appliqué page, trace around each appliqué shape onto the paper side of the fusible webbing (Bondaweb/Wonderweb).
Cut out the shapes roughly - **do not** cut out accurately along the lines at this stage. Following the manufacturer's instructions iron the fusible cut-outs onto the WRONG side of the relevant fabrics. The sheep and lamb bodies should be fused onto felt.
Tip: If you are using white cotton fabric instead of felt for the bodies you can fuse two pieces of fabric together to create a thicker fabric. This will stop the background showing through.

3.   Allow to cool then cut out the shapes accurately along the traced lines.   Peel the paper from each shape. Position all pieces onto the mug rug top as shown in the photo and on the appliqué page. Tuck the top of the feet, head and tail under the bodies. When happy with the placement, iron to fuse the pieces in place.
Note: You may find it easier to fuse and stitch the heart to the blanket before fusing it to the sheep's body in which case you should not remove the paper from the sheep until the blankets have been fused in place.

4.   Hand or machine stitch the shapes in place. Create the eyes using two strands of white cotton and a French knot or a simple overstitch.   Add any additional stitching as preferred.
I added tails to both lambs using two strands of black embroidery cotton.

5.   Lay the backing 11" x 7" rectangle, **wrong** side facing up and place the batting on top. Position the appliquéd mug rug centrally on top with **right** side facing up. Baste or pin all three layers together, ensuring that the backing and top remain flat and smooth. Quilt around the sheep and lambs and add any additional quilting as desired.

6.   Once all quilting has been completed, trim backing and batting to the same size as the mug rug top.

7.   Bind the mug rug using the binding method of your choice.
I used a 1¼" wide single-fold binding.
(See 'Binding' in General Instructions.)

11

SPRING CHICKEN MUG RUG
(Finished size: 9" x 5½")

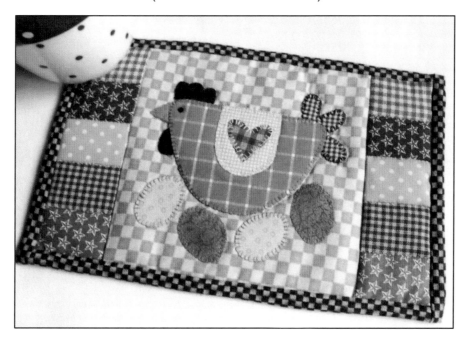

Eggs are the symbol of new beginnings whilst the chicken signifies homely comfort.
Combine the two and you have the perfect spot for your tea and cake.

Fabric Requirement:

For the Background:
One 6" x 5½" rectangle
Five 1½" x 4" strips from different fabrics

For the Chicken:
One 4" x 5" rectangle for the body
Scraps of red fabric/felt for wattle/comb
Scrap of yellow fabric/felt for beak

For the Eggs:
Four 2" squares

You will also need:
Scraps of fabric for blanket, heart and tail feathers
One 11" x 8" rectangle of cotton fabric for backing
One 11" x 8" rectangle of lightweight batting
8" square fusible webbing   (i.e. Bondaweb/Wonderweb)
1 yard of 1¼" binding fabric (i.e. bias binding or cotton strips)
Stranded Embroidery Cotton

Mug Rug Construction

1.   With right sides together stitch the five 1½" x 4" strips together along the 4" length as shown below. Unit should measure 5½ x 4". Press.

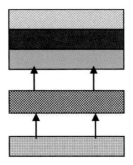

2.   Cut this unit in half to create two 5½ x 2" strips. Press.

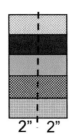

2"   2"

3.   Stitch a 2" side strip to each side of the central rectangle. Press. The mug rug top should measure 9" x 5½".

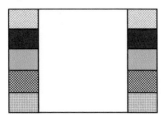

4.   From the appliqué page, trace around each appliqué shape onto the paper side of the fusible webbing (Bondaweb/Wonderweb).
Note: The chicken has been reversed on the appliqué page – trace all pieces exactly as they appear – they will be right way round on the mug rug.

5.   Cut out the shapes roughly - **do not** cut out accurately along the lines at this stage. Following the manufacturer's instructions iron the fusible webbing cut-outs onto the WRONG side of your chosen fabrics.

6.   Allow to cool then cut out the shapes accurately along the traced lines.   Peel the paper from each shape. Position all pieces onto the mug rug as shown in the photo and on the appliqué page. Leave **at least** ¼" between the appliqué pieces and the edge of the mug rug. When happy with the placement, iron to fuse the pieces in place.
Tip: If you are hand stitching the appliqué you may find it easier to fuse and stitch the heart to the blanket before fusing it to the chicken. In this case do not remove the backing paper from the chicken until you have fused the blanket in place.

7.   Hand or machine stitch the shapes in place. The eye of the chicken is made using two strands of black embroidery thread and a simple overstitch. Add any additional stitching as desired.

8.   Lay the 11" x 8" backing rectangle, **wrong** side facing up and place the batting on top. Position the appliquéd mug rug centrally on top with **right** side facing up. Baste or pin all three layers together, ensuring that the backing and top remain flat and smooth. Quilt around the chicken and add any additional quilting as desired.
I quilted in the ditch on all seams.

9.   Once all quilting has been completed, trim backing and batting to the same size as the mug rug top.

10.   Bind the mug rug using the binding method of your choice *(see 'Binding' in General Instructions).*
I used a 1¼" single-fold binding.

15

SCOTTIE DOGS MUG RUG

(Finished size: 9½" x 5")

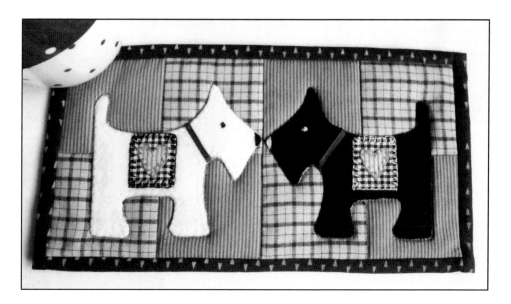

You don't need to be a dog lover to enjoy this nose-to-tail mug rug – all you need is a little bit of felt and sewing thread. To save time you could replace the neck ribbon with a couple of rows of chain stitch and leave off the hearts.
No matter how you create this functional mini quilt one thing is certain, these two Scottie dogs will always see eye-to-eye.

Fabric Requirements:

For the Background:
One 9½" x 5" rectangle **OR** eight 2¾" squares of fabric

For the Scottie Dogs:
One 5" square of black felt or cotton fabric
One 5" square of white felt or thick cotton fabric

You will also need:
Scraps of fabric for the coats and hearts
4" length of ⅛"-¼" wide ribbon for collars (optional)
One 11" x 7" rectangle of cotton fabric for backing
One 11" x 7" rectangle of lightweight batting
8" square fusible webbing   (i.e. Bondaweb/Wonderweb)
1 yard of 1¼" binding fabric (i.e. bias binding or cotton strips)
Stranded Embroidery Cotton

Mug Rug Construction

1.   If you are patching the background stitch eight 2¾" squares, right sides together as shown, to make a patched 9½" x 5" rectangle. Press.

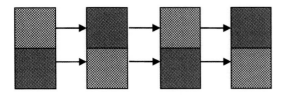

Tip: Do not worry if your seams do not match exactly as the Scottie Dogs will lie on top of most of them.

2.   From the appliqué page, trace around each appliqué shape onto the paper side of the fusible webbing (Bondaweb). Cut out the shapes roughly - do not cut out accurately at this stage. Following the manufacturer's instructions iron the fusible webbing cut-outs onto the WRONG side of the relevant fabrics.

3.   Allow to cool then cut out the shapes accurately along the traced lines before peeling off the backing paper.
Tip: *If you wish to add coats to the dogs then you may find it easier to appliqué the coats to each dog before you fuse them to the mug rug top – this will reduce the number of layers you need to sew through. In this case do not remove the backing paper from the Scottie Dogs until you have fused the blankets in place.*

4.   Using the appliqué page as a guide, position the dogs onto the front of the background rectangle. Make sure that they are at least ½" away from the edge of the mug rug. When happy with the arrangement, iron to fuse in place. Hand or machine stitch around each appliqué shape (I used a simple blanket stitch).

5.   Add thin ribbon for the collars if desired. Stitch an eye and nose onto each dog using a simple overstitch and two strands of black embroidery thread. *Alternatively you could replace this ribbon collar with a chain-stitch collar.*

6.   Lay the backing 11" x 7" rectangle, **wrong** side facing up and place the batting on top. Position the appliquéd mug rug centrally on top with **right** side facing up. Pin the three layers together, ensuring that the backing and top remain flat and smooth. Quilt around each shape and add any decorative stitches or quilting as preferred.

7.   Once all quilting has been completed, trim backing and batting to the same size as the mug rug top.

8.   Bind the mug rug using the binding method of your choice (*see 'Binding' in General Instructions for examples of binding methods*).
I used a 1¼" single-fold binding.

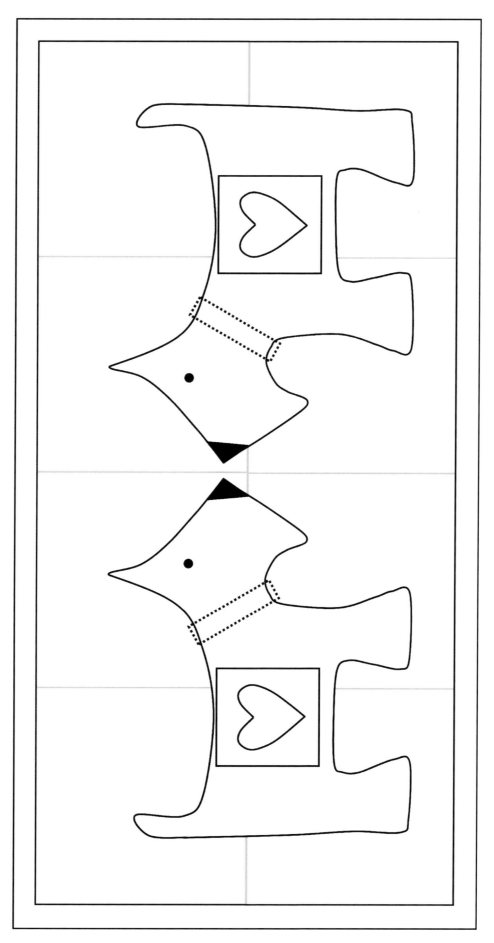

19

RED ELEPHANTS MUG RUG

(Finished size: 8½" x 4½")

You will never forget where you put your cup and cookie with this charming mug rug. Ideal for when space is limited, this whimsical mini quilt will look just as good on the coffee table as it would in a child's room. But remember, not all elephants have red ears – some have turquoise, paisley or polka dot ears!

Fabric Requirements:

For the Background:
One 8½" x 4½" rectangle **OR** eight 2½" squares of fabric

For the Elephants:
One 5" square of grey fabric or felt

You will also need:
Scraps of patterned fabric for ears and hearts
One 10" x 6" rectangle of cotton fabric for backing
One 10" x 6" rectangle of lightweight batting
8" square fusible webbing   (i.e. Bondaweb/Wonderweb)
1 yard of 1¼" binding fabric (i.e. bias binding or cotton strips)
Stranded Embroidery Cotton

Mug Rug Construction

1.   If patching the mug rug top stitch eight 2½" squares together to make a patched rectangle 8½" x 4½" as shown. Press.

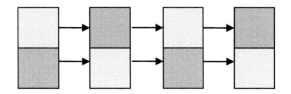

2.   From the appliqué page, trace around each appliqué shape onto the paper side of the fusible webbing (Bondaweb). Trace the shapes **exactly** as shown – they have been reversed so that the baby elephant will be on the left-hand side of the finished mug rug. Cut out the shapes roughly - **do not** cut out accurately at this stage.

3.   Following the manufacturer's instructions iron the fusible webbing cut-outs onto the WRONG side of the relevant fabrics.
Tip: If you have a dark background fabric you can fuse two pieces of grey fabric together and use as one piece for the elephants. This will stop the background showing through.

4.   Allow to cool before cutting out accurately along the traced lines. Peel the paper from each shape taking care not to pull the elephants out of shape.

5.   Using the appliqué page as a guide position the two elephants onto the front of the mug rug rectangle ensuring each elephant is at least ½" away from the edge of the mug rug. Position the ears on top and the hearts above the trunks. When happy with the arrangement, iron to fuse the pieces in place.

6.   Hand or machine stitch around each appliqué shape (I used a simple blanket stitch). Add an eye to each elephant using two strands of black embroidery thread and a very small overstitch.

7.   Lay the backing 10" x 6" rectangle, **wrong** side facing up and place the batting on top. Position the appliquéd mug rug centrally on top with **right** side facing up. Baste or pin all three layers together, ensuring that the backing and top remain flat and smooth. Quilt around each shape.

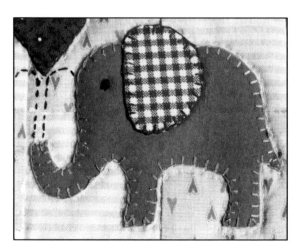

8.   Create water spouts using a simple running stitch. You can do this by hand using two strands of embroidery thread or by machine. Add any additional quilting as preferred.

9.   Once all quilting has been completed, trim backing and batting to the same size as the mug rug top.

10.   Bind the mug rug using the binding method of your choice *(see 'Binding' in General Instructions for examples of binding methods).*
I used a 1¼" single fold binding.

WHALES MUG RUG
(Finished size: 9" x 5½")

Big and bold, these whales like nothing more than to protect your table from spills and splashes. The wave is created using a simple strip applique method – great for using up scraps of fabric or left-over binding strips.

Fabric Requirements:

For the Background:
One 9" x 4¼" 'sky' rectangle
One 9" x 1¾" 'sea' rectangle

For the Wave:
A selection of 3" strips varying in width between 1" and 1½"

For the Whales:
One 6" square of grey linen or fabric

You will also need:
Fabric scraps for hearts and eyes.
One 11" x 7" rectangle of cotton fabric for backing
One 11" x 7" rectangle of lightweight batting
10" x 6" rectangle fusible webbing   (i.e. Bondaweb/Wonderweb)
1 yard of 1¼" binding fabric (i.e. bias binding or cotton strips)
Stranded Embroidery Cotton

Mug Rug Construction

1.   With right sides together stitch the two background rectangles together along the 9" length to create a mug rug top measuring 9" x 5½". Press.

2.   Construct the wave block by stitching the various strips together along the 3" length until you have created a rectangle which is at least 9½" long. Press.
Tip: Shorten your stitch length when sewing the strips together – this will stop the wave pulling apart when you appliqué it into position. Alternatively you can use one 2½" x 9½" rectangle of fabric.

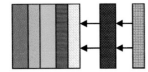

3.   Trace around all shapes from the appliqué page onto the paper side of the fusible webbing.
Note: The whales have been reversed – trace exactly as shown – they will be the right way round on the finished mug rug.

4.   Cut out the shapes roughly - **do not** cut out accurately along the traced lines at this stage. Following the manufacturer's instructions iron the fusible webbing cut-outs onto the WRONG side of your chosen fabrics. The wave cut-out should be fused to the wrong side of the wave block created at step 2 above.

5.   Allow to cool then cut out the shapes accurately along the traced lines.   Peel the paper from each shape being careful not to pull the seams apart on the wave block.

6.   Position the two whales onto the front of the mug rug so that they lie close to the sea/sky seam. The wave should lie partially on top of the two whales and cover the seam completely. Use the appliqué page and photo as a guide. Ensure that the whales and the hearts are **at least ½"** from the edge of the mug rug to allow for binding. When happy with the layout, iron to fuse in place.

7.   Stitch the appliqué pieces in place by hand or machine.

8.   Appliqué the whales' eyes in place. Alternatively you could embroider them using two strands of black embroidery thread and a simple overstitch. .Add water spouts using two strands of embroidery thread and a running stitch.
Tip: If you prefer the water spouts can be quilted in place when quilting the mug rug.

9.   Lay the 11" x 7" backing rectangle, **wrong** side facing up and place the batting on top. Position the mug rug centrally on top with **right** side facing up. Baste or pin all three layers together, ensuring that the backing and top remain flat and smooth. Quilt around all appliqué shapes. Add any further quilting as desired.
I shadow quilted the sea below the wave and quilted in the ditch at the top of the wave.

10.   Once all quilting has been completed, trim backing and batting to the same size as the mug rug top.

11.   Bind the mug rug using the binding method of your choice *(see 'Binding' in General Instructions for examples of binding methods).*
I used a 1¼" wide single-fold binding.

FOX MUG RUG and COASTER
(Finished mug rug size: 9" x 5½" – Finished coaster size: 4½")

Seek out those leaf prints as they will provide the perfect backdrop for this wily fox as he sits amongst the toadstools, looking out for your tea and cookie.
Of course, your fox doesn't have to be a traditional red or brown fox – you might prefer a purple or black fox instead.

Fabric Requirements:
For the Background:
One 9" x 5½" rectangle

For the Fox:
One 5" square of linen/cotton for the body
One 3" square of linen/cotton for the head
One 4" square of thick white linen/cotton or felt for the tail and face
Small piece of black felt for the nose

You will also need::
Scraps for the toadstools
One 11" x 7" rectangle of cotton fabric for backing
One 11" x 7" rectangle of lightweight batting
8" square of fusible webbing   (i.e. Bondaweb)
1 yard of 1¼" binding fabric (i.e. bias binding or cotton strips)
Co-ordinating thread

Fabric requirements for the coaster are provided with the instructions.

Mug Rug Construction

1.   From the appliqué page, trace around all appliqué shapes onto the paper side of the fusible webbing. Cut out the shapes roughly - do not cut out accurately at this stage.

2.   Following the manufacturer's instructions, iron the fusible cut-outs onto the WRONG side of your chosen fabric. The face and tail should be fused onto thick cotton, linen or felt.
Tip: If you do not have thick cotton you can fuse two 4" squares together and treat as one piece. This will stop the background fabric showing through.

3.   Allow to cool then cut out the shapes accurately along the traced lines.   Peel the paper from each piece and position the fabric shapes onto the mug rug background as shown on the appliqué page.
Tip: If hand stitching you may find it easier to fuse and stitch the face to the head before fusing the head onto the mug rug. If so do not remove the backing paper from the head until after you have fused the face in place.
All pieces should be ½" away from the edge of the background rectangle to allow for the binding.   When happy with the arrangement, iron to fuse the shapes in place.
Note: *Tuck the bottom of the ears under the head.*

4.   Stitch each shape in place by hand or machine.

5.   Create the eyes using two strands of black embroidery thread and a simple overstitch (*I used 5 stitches for each eye with one long stitch across the top*).
The nose is created from

a small scrap of black felt. Shape the felt into a small triangle and stitch in place. *Alternatively you can embroider a nose using two strands of black embroidery cotton.*

6.   Lay the 11" x 7" backing rectangle, **wrong** side facing up and place the batting on top. Position the mug rug centrally on top with **right** side facing up. Baste or pin all three layers together, ensuring that the backing and top remain flat and smooth.

7.   Quilt around each shape by hand or machine. Add any additional quilting as desired.
I shadow quilted curved lines onto the fox's body.

8.   Once all quilting has been completed, press the mug rug and trim the backing and batting to the same size as the mug rug top.

9.   Bind the mug rug using the binding method of your choice *(see 'Binding' in General Instructions for examples of binding methods).*
I used a 1¼" wide single fold binding.

COASTER

To make one coaster you will need:

Two 6" squares for front and back
One 3" square for the head
One 4" square of white fabric/felt
One 6" square of batting

30

C1.   Cut two 5" circles from cotton fabric using the template below.

C2.   Follow steps 1-5 of the pattern to appliqué the fox's head and tail to the RIGHT side of one of the 5" circles of fabric. Remember to leave **at least** ¼" space between the appliqué and the edge of the circle.   Add the eyes and nose as detailed in step 5.

C3.   Once the fox's head and tail are complete lay the backing circle, **right side facing up**, on top of the batting square. Place the appliquéd circle, **right side facing down**, on top of both. Baste or pin all three layers together.

C4.   Stitch the circles together using a ¼" seam allowance. Leave a 1½" gap unstitched for turning through.

C5.   Trim the batting so that it is slightly smaller than the two fabric circles before turning the coaster, right side out. Press.

C6.   Slip-stitch the opening closed and add quilting as desired.
(*I quilted curves around the body and added detail to the tail.*)

31

32

HEDGEHOGS MUG RUG
(Finished size: 8½" x 5")

Happy to curl up in a clump of leaves, cosy and warm, these little chaps are just as content lying underneath a warm mug or cup.
As for those spikes – they are nothing more than cross-stitches. No prickles here!

<u>Fabric Requirements</u>:
For the Background:
One 8½" x 4" rectangle
One 8½" x 1½" rectangle (*this could be patched if preferred*)

For the Hedgehogs:
Two 4" squares for the bodies
Two 2" squares for the faces and feet

You will also need:
Scraps of fabric for the appliqué leaves
A small scrap of black felt for hedgehog noses
One 10" x 7" rectangle of cotton fabric for backing
One 10" x 7" rectangle of lightweight batting
8" square of fusible webbing for appliqué (i.e. Wonderweb)
1 yard of 1¼" binding fabric (i.e. bias binding/cotton strips)
Stranded Embroidery Cotton for hand appliqué

Mug Rug Construction

1.   With RIGHT sides together stitch the two background rectangles together to make an 8½" x 5" mug rug top. Press.

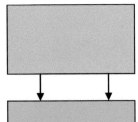

2.   From the appliqué page trace all shapes onto the paper side of the fusible webbing (Wonderweb). Cut out the shapes roughly - do not cut out accurately along the traced lines at this stage. Following the manufacturer's instructions iron the fusible webbing cut-outs onto the WRONG side of your chosen fabrics. The noses should be fused onto felt due to their size – this will make them easier to stitch in place.

3.   Allow to cool then cut out the shapes accurately along the traced lines. Peel the paper from each shape. Using the appliqué page and photo as a guide, position the two hedgehogs and four leaves onto the mug rug top. The hedgehog bodies lie on top of the feet and face. Ensure you leave at least ¼" between the appliqué pieces and the edge of the mug rug to allow for the binding. When happy with the arrangement, iron to fuse in place. Stitch each piece in place by hand or machine.

4.   Use two strands of embroidery cotton create a row of cross stitches along the back of each hedgehog to represent the hedgehog spikes. Do not pull your cross stitching too tight but try to keep it flat. You may find that the stitches naturally pull together very slightly – this is okay and will add definition to the hedgehogs.

5.   Create the hedgehog eyes using two strands of black embroidery cotton and a simple overstitch or a French knot. Add any additional stitching as desired. *I added detail to each leaf.*

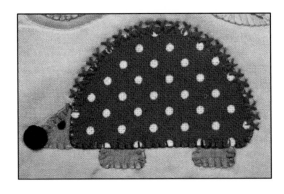

6.   Lay the 10" x 7" backing rectangle, **wrong** side facing up and place the batting on top. Position the appliquéd mug rug centrally on top with **right** side facing up. Pin the three layers together. Quilt as desired. *I outline quilted around the leaves and hedgehogs. I also quilted in the ditch between the two rectangles before adding wind swirls along the bottom rectangle as indicated by the dashed lines on the appliqué page.*

7.   Once all quilting has been completed, trim backing and batting to the same size as the mug rug top.

8.   Bind the mug rug using the binding method of your choice *(see* 'Binding' in General Instructions for examples of binding methods). *I used a 1¼" wide single-fold binding.*

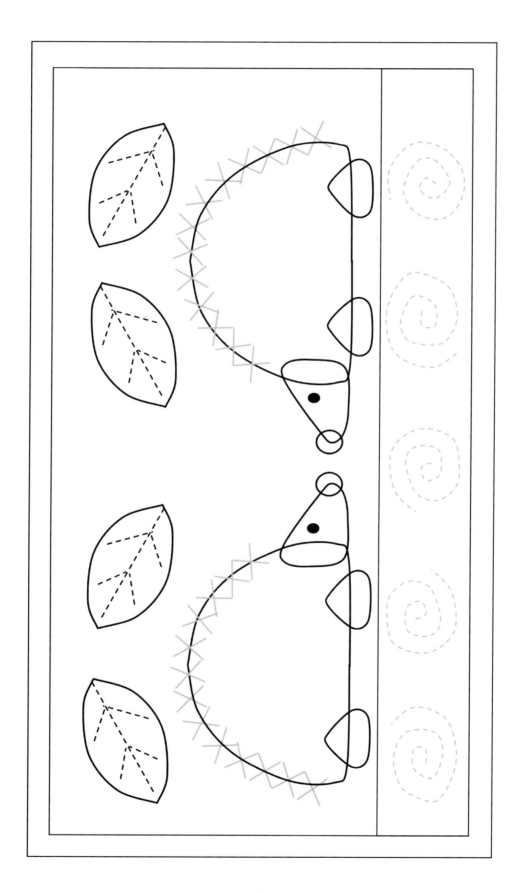

BLACK & WHITE CATS MUG RUG

(Finished size: 8½" x 5")

Chasing mice or catching fish – these are two very cute cats.
When they are not playing they will be happy to sit on your table - protecting the
surface from drips and drops.   Take your time with the little pieces of this mug rug and
you will be rewarded with a purrfect mini quilt.

Fabric Requirements:

For the Background:
Two 4" x 5" rectangles
One 1½" x 5" rectangle

For the Cats:
Two 4" x 3" rectangles for cat bodies
One 3" x 7" rectangle for face and tails
One 1½" square of felt for the cats' eyes

You will also need:
Scraps of fabric for the bird, fish or mouse
One 10" x 7" rectangle of cotton fabric for backing
One 10" x 7" rectangle of lightweight batting
8" square of fusible webbing for appliqué (i.e. Wonderweb)
1 yard of 1¼" binding fabric (i.e. bias binding or cotton strips)
Stranded Embroidery Cotton

Mug Rug Construction

1.   Make the background by stitching the two 4" x 5" rectangles to either side of the 1½" x 5" central strip as shown to make an 8½" x 5" background rectangle.

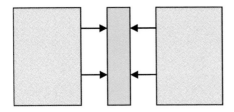

Note: For the cat-and-fish mug rug I patched the background rectangles from two 4" x 2⅜" rectangles.

2.   From the appliqué page trace all shapes onto the paper side of the fusible webbing (Wonderweb). *Note: The small bird has been reversed – trace it exactly as it is shown – it will be the right way round on the finished mug rug.*

3.   Cut out the shapes roughly - **do not** cut out accurately along the traced lines at this stage. Following the manufacturer's instructions iron the fusible webbing cut-outs onto the WRONG side of your chosen fabrics.

4.   Allow to cool then cut out the shapes accurately along the traced lines.   Peel the paper from each shape.

5.   Using the appliqué page and photo as a guide, position the two cats, bird and mouse/fish onto the 8½" x 5" background rectangle. Ensure you leave at least ¼" between the appliqué pieces and the edge of the mug rug to allow for the binding. When happy with the arrangement, iron to fuse in place.

6.   Hand or machine stitch each piece in place.
I hand appliquéd the mouse and fish using just one strand of embroidery cotton – this minimises the impact of the stitching.

7.   Add stitching detail to the cats' ears and mouth using two strands of embroidery cotton and a simple running stitch. Add a tail to the mouse in the same way. The bird's beak, cats' nose and all eyes are made by overstitching a small stitch in place using two strands of embroidery cotton. Add whiskers to both cats by hand or machine.

8.   Lay the 10" x 7" backing rectangle, **wrong** side facing up and place the batting on top. Position the appliquéd mug rug centrally on top with **right** side facing up. Pin the three layers together. Outline quilt around the cats. Add any additional quilting as preferred.

9.   Once all quilting has been completed, trim backing and batting to the same size as the mug rug top.

10.   Bind the mug rug using the binding method of your choice *(see 'Binding' in General Instructions for examples of binding methods).*
I used a 1¼" wide mitred binding.

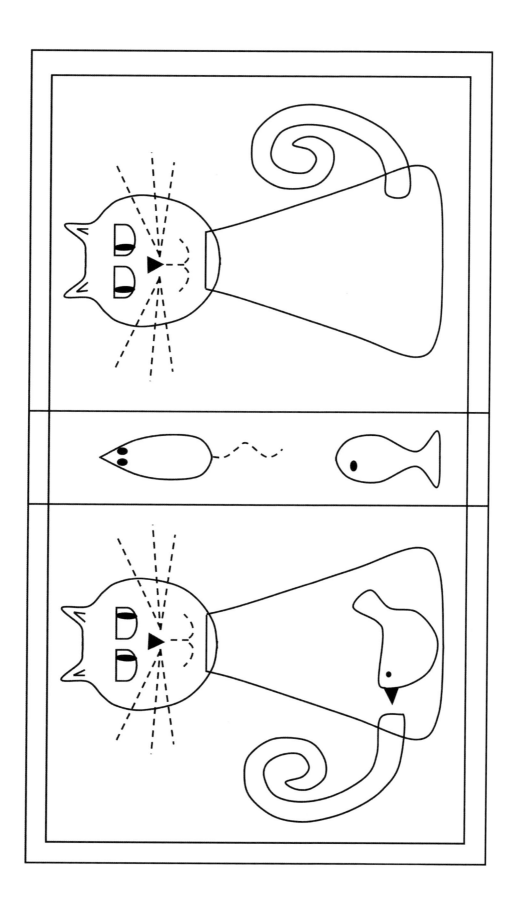

39

TWO OWLS MUG RUG
(Finished size: 9" x 5½")

Owls are such wise old birds and these two are no exception.   They know how to make a table look inviting and how to make a home look cosy. Follow the tips throughout the pattern and you can make your very own version or twooooooo!

Fabric Requirements:
For the Background:
One 9" x 3¼" rectangle
One 9" x 2¼" rectangle
One 9" x 1" branch strip

For the Owls:
Two 4" squares for the bodies
Two 3" squares for the wings
Scraps of felt for eyes and beaks

For the Leaves:
One 4" square for the leaves
One 4" square for the flower petals
One 2" square for the flower middles

You will also need:
Scraps of fabric for the bird and bird nest.
One 11" x 7" rectangle of fabric for backing
One 11" x 7" rectangle of lightweight batting
10" square fusible webbing   (i.e. Bondaweb/Wonderweb)
1 yard of 1¼" binding fabric (i.e. bias binding or cotton strips)
Stranded Embroidery Cotton

Mug Rug Construction

1.   Create the mug rug top by stitching the two background rectangles to the branch rectangle as shown. Mug rug top should measure 9" x 5½". Press.

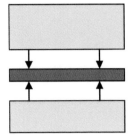

2.   From the appliqué page, trace around each appliqué shape onto the paper side of the fusible webbing (Bondaweb/Wonderweb). Cut out the shapes roughly - **do not** cut out accurately at this stage.
Note: The small bird in the nest has been reversed. Trace exactly as shown - they will be the right way round once you have fused them in place.

3.   Following the manufacturer's instructions iron the fusible cut-outs onto the WRONG side of the relevant fabrics. The eyes and beaks should be fused onto felt; this will make it easier to appliqué them.

4.   Allow the shapes to cool before cutting out accurately along the traced lines.   Peel the paper from each shape.

5.   Position all pieces onto the mug rug as shown on the appliqué page. Tuck the top of the feet under the owls' bodies and the little bird under the nest.
TIP: Take your time with this step; I placed the appliqué page on the ironing board alongside the mug rug top. You may find it easier to fuse and stitch the owls in place before adding the flowers, leaves and bird nest.

6.   When happy with the placement, iron to fuse the pieces in place. Hand or machine stitch all shapes in place.

7.   Decide whether you want the owls looking straight ahead or at each other and create the eyes using two strands of black cotton and a simple overstitch. Add stems and stitching detail to the leaves if desired.

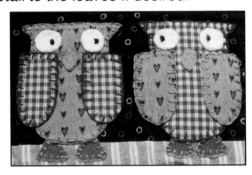

8.   The beak of the small bird-in-the-nest is created using two strands of yellow cotton stitched in a triangle shape. Add an eye in black thread. Do not worry if your stitching is uneven as it will add to the country charm.

9.   Lay the 11" x 7" backing rectangle, **wrong** side facing up and place the batting on top. Position the appliquéd mug rug centrally on top with **right** side facing up. Baste or pin all three layers together, ensuring that the backing and top remain flat and smooth. Quilt around the owls, branch, flowers and leaves.   Add any additional quilting as desired.
Tip: The closer you outline quilt to the shapes the more they will puff up.

10.   Once all quilting has been completed, trim backing and batting to the same size as the mug rug top.

11.   Bind the mug rug using the binding method of your choice *(see 'Binding' in General Instructions for examples of binding methods).*
I used a 1¼" wide mitred binding.

CHRISTMAS ANTLERS MUG RUG
(Finished size: 9" x 6")

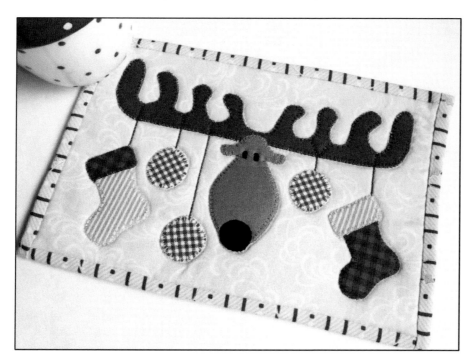

Who needs a tree when there are such antlers to be found?
This little mug rug makes a welcome addition to the Christmas table. Make one to keep
and one to give and share the pleasure of these functional little mini quilts.

Fabric Requirements:
For the Background:
One 9" x 6" rectangle

For the Reindeer
One 2½" x 9" rectangle for the antlers
One 3" x 4" rectangle for the head
One 1½" square of felt/fabric for the nose

For the Baubles and Stockings:
One 3" square each from different fabrics for the stockings
One 4" square for the baubles

You will also need:
One 11" x 8" rectangle of cotton fabric for backing
One 11" x 8" rectangle of lightweight batting
9" square fusible webbing   (i.e. Bondaweb/Wonderweb)
1 yard of 1¼" binding fabric (i.e. bias binding or cotton strips)
Stranded embroidery thread

Mug Rug Construction

1.   Trace around all shapes from the appliqué page, onto the paper side of the fusible webbing.
Note: the stockings have been reversed – trace them exactly as shown.

2.   Cut out the shapes roughly leaving approximately ¼" around each tracing. **Do not** cut out accurately along the traced lines at this stage.

3.   Following the manufacturer's instructions iron the fusible webbing cut-outs onto the WRONG side of your chosen fabrics.
Tip: I used felt for the nose – this makes it easier to stitch.

4.   Allow to cool completely before cutting out all shapes accurately along the traced lines. Remove the paper from each shape.

5.   Using the appliqué page as a guide and ensuring all pieces are at least ½" away from the edge of the mug rug, position the antlers and head onto the front of the background rectangle. The head should lie on top of the antlers.

6.   Position each bauble and stocking so that the hanging thread will hang between antler horns with the exception of the bauble on the right-hand side – this bauble is positioned between horns with a 'v' thread as shown on the appliqué page.

7.   When happy with the arrangement, iron to fuse in place. Stitch the shapes in position by hand or machine.
Tip: *You will find it easier to fuse and stitch the head before adding the nose.*

8.   Create the eyes using two strands of black embroidery thread and a simple overstitch.

9.   Lay the 11" x 8" backing rectangle, **wrong** side facing up and place the batting on top. Position the appliquéd mug rug centrally on top with **right** side facing up. Pin the three layers together, ensuring that the backing and top remain flat and smooth. Quilt around all pieces.

10.   Stitch the hanging threads by hand or machine, so that they run from the top of the stockings and baubles, up to the antlers as indicated by the dashed lines on the appliqué page.
I used four lines of machine stitching to create each hanging thread.

11.   Add any additional quilting or stitching as desired.

12.   Once all quilting has been completed, trim backing and batting to the same size as the mug rug top.

13.   Bind the mug rug using the binding method of your choice *(see 'Binding' in General Instructions for examples of binding methods).*
I used a 1¼" wide single fold binding.

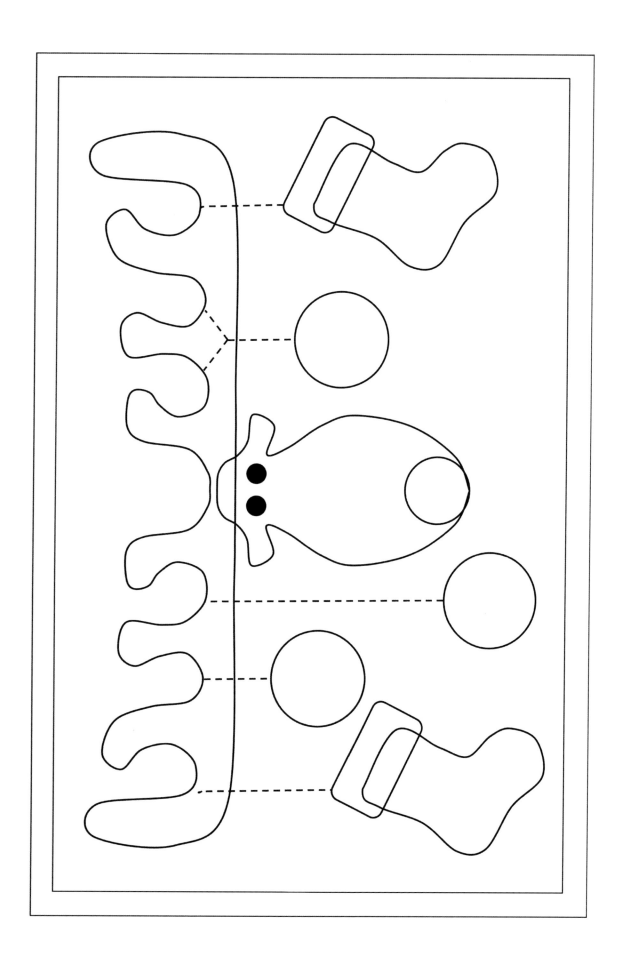

ABOUT THE AUTHOR

I am Amanda Weatherill, also known as the Patchsmith. I live in a little village nestled in the Hampshire countryside where I spend my days designing and making mini quilts - they are my hobby and my passion. My philosophy is simple – share this passion so that everybody has the opportunity to create a little piece of fabric art for their home. Mug rugs are the perfect way to achieve this. Using little more than scraps of fabric you too can enjoy the hobby of mug rug making to create something unique and functional for your desk or table. In so doing you will always have a reminder close to hand of your love of fabric, fun and colour.

Join me as I share my quick and easy designs to help you create a life full of fabric, fun and friends.

You can find the Patchsmith on Facebook, Flickr, Pinterest and Instagram.

To find out more about Patchsmith patterns and mug rug making visit **thepatchsmith.blogspot.co.uk**.

29812973R00031

Printed in Great Britain
by Amazon